High Praise for
COURBET'S BLUE PARROT
by Stephen Fife

HURT PEOPLE HURT people. But sometimes, hurt people juggle irreverence & profundity, pain, yearning, love, lust, and arrested adolescence with great empathy, humor, and live nude irreconcilable truth. Stephen Fife, who completed his 10,000 hours decades ago, is one such hurt person -- a life-wisened, hopelessly romantic funny sonuvabitch -- and his poetry, which in this edition span 50 years of writing, is wise, crack-potted, occasionally elegant, often profound and always effortlessly readable and human.

> STEPHEN ADLY GUIRGIS, playwright, winner of The Pulitzer Prize

STEPHEN FIFE'S *Courbert's Blue Parrot* is filled with deeply personal poetry that was clearly painful for the poet to access as he struggles to sum up the meaning of what he went through in his life, what he felt when he did and most importantly, what he lost.

> RICHARD VETERE, author, *The Writers Afterlife* and *Champagne and Cocaine*

I LOVED THE passionate young artist feasting on the exquisite pain of poetry to sustain and explain himself amidst the whirlings of his life.

> BILLY HAYES, author of the best-selling *Midnight Express*

WITH THESE BRAVE poems, Stephen Fife transforms meditations on day-to-day life into searing art. Part cinema verite, part confessional dramas reported from the front lines of love, this raw new writing has the ring of truth.

> —JOHN SHEA, actor/writer/producer

DRAWING FROM SUCH poets as D.H. Lawrence and Charles Bukowski, Fife encourages us to awaken the part of ourselves we want to be again. This book is about what the world has forgotten: that poetry saves our ass.

> WENDY OXENHORN, a.k.a. The Barefoot Baroness

A TERRIFIC SELECTION of work, some aware youthful short. Often about sex and how it can be a wonder of the world. And then longer, short stories as poems, never not a poem, a distillation of experience and always, you feel, truthful but truth seen through the artist's eyes and mind. . . And more than once the unforgettable line or remark or image.

> MICHAEL LINDSAY-HOGG, actor/director

Courbet's Blue Parrot

Courbet's Blue Parrot

POEMS OF LOVE AND SEX

BY

STEPHEN FIFE

ShiftPoetry™
PRESS

Courbet's Blue Parrot: Poems of Love and Sex
BY Stephen Fife

Introduction © Stephen Fife 2021
All poems © Stephen Fife 2021

Cover designed by: © Yuval Shrem

Cover image:
© Detail from *Woman with A Parrot* (1866) by Gustave Courbet,
in the collection of the Metropolitan Museum, New York City.

Thanks to Scott Davis and Cune Press for permission to reprint the following poems
from *DREAMING IN THE MAZE OF LOVE-GRIEF-MADNESS* (Cune Press, 2014):
*One, Invocation, The Wilting Rose, The Importer of Love, Women and Water, Balloon, Maria Victoria,
What Happened, Elegy for a Lost Love, The Lover, Night Thoughts, The Kiss at 6 AM, Everything Looks
Beautiful in the Morning, Poem!*

Thanks to Scott Davis and Cune Press for permission to reprint
the following poems from *TWISTED HIPSTER* (Cune Press, 2015):
Home, Remembering U, School Dance, My Night with Carla, Background Noise, Goddess.

Several of the new poems originated in sessions of ShiftPoetry™, a program developed and
run by Howard Kern and Barbara Ligeti.

ISBN 978-1-7348787-2-1 (trade paperback original)
First edition published January 2022

BOOK DESIGN:
KG Design International
www.katgeorges.com
kgeokat@mac.com

ShiftPoetry Press
910 West End Avenue Suite 6F
New York, New York 10025
www.ShiftPoetry.com

To CLK, my favorite nurse

and Corona companion.

"Last night I woke up with someone squeezing my hand.

It was my other hand."

—William Burroughs—

TABLE OF CONTENTS

CONTENTS *(continued)*

INTRODUCTION

I have been reading a lot of poetry lately by women in their 20s and 30s, and much of it is very exciting, full of strong feelings, deep questions, conflicts and contradictions. Most of the best work has been from women of color or women from immigrant groups traditionally excluded from having a prominent voice in mainstream culture. They articulate difficult and heartrending challenges to an unjust society, asking, "Where do I belong in this world? How can I be my authentic self in the midst of so much hypocrisy, in the midst of so much toxicity and bullshit?"

I can relate. Even though I come from the mainstream—a Jewish man from a well-to-do family, educated in prep school and Liberal Arts and Ivy League universities—I see my life as being a quest for answers to those questions too. The one condition needed for a writer to keep growing is Freedom—the freedom to make choices, the freedom to stay creatively open, the freedom to fail—and that is the most difficult thing to hold onto as one grows older. Nowhere more so than where questions of love and sex are concerned.

But life is desire and desire is life, and love and sex are going to happen whether the arbiters of the socially acceptable like it or not. The fact that folks over 50—and 60! And 70!—still have active libidos and fantasy lives may seem horrifying to some and a source of inspiration to others. Either way, things will continue to happen, and people will try to find happiness.

My blessing on all those who act out of love without resorting to exploitation. It's not easy to be human in this world, not easy to treat other humans with the same respect that we want for ourselves. But it is a quest very much worth undertaking.

—Steve F in sunny SoCal

PREFACE
POEM

SERENDIPITY

Serendipity
Might be my religion
Or as close to a religion
As I will ever have.

So when I find myself
On a train that bypasses my stop
And takes me somewhere that
I wasn't planning to go,
Then I look around after getting off
Wondering:
Is there any reason I'm here?
Is there anything here that
Otherwise I might not have found?

You can call this simply a wish
For logic from the universe,
However hidden, however opaque.
You can call this simply a hope
That chance is working in my favor,
That chance has some hidden purpose for me.
However, this is how I found my only child,
At one of these unforeseen stops.
This is how she got born.

Because I was supposed to be downtown
At a party that evening, joining a woman
There who I had been going out with.
But it had been raining all day, and the
Stations were flooded, and the trains weren't
Running. It was the nineties in New York City,
So neither of us had cell phones, and I couldn't

Let her know what was going on. By the time
I got to the party she was so angry that she
Wouldn't speak with me. So I ended up
Speaking with a beautiful woman with long
Red hair who turned out to be funny and to have
The same literary agent as I did.

And three years later
The two of us had a daughter.
Which rhymes with "All that water."
Without which she would not be around.

So is it any wonder that Serendipity
Is like my religion? Just look where it got me.

Courbet's
Blue Parrot

EARLY

POEMS

ONE

Hold me closer than the night
Shield me from the shadowed dark
Feel my warmth against wind's bite –
Know we two are not alone
For we are love and love is one.

Love is one, yes, love is one –
That is the theme of all our songs,
The summary of all we've done
And all that we aspire to do –
There is no me, there is no you,

There is not even us – there is only
Love, a place where we can always run
To find each other, where loneli-
ness cannot exist, as long as we are one.

Written 1970.

INVOCATION

Back beneath the shadow
Of your hand,
Back beneath the shadow
Of our early doom

And the room in which Prince Hamlet
Cracked the eggshell of his infant brain
And entered out of darkness
To be dark again;

Back before the breathing time of pain
When a ball of twine lay cradled
Among the complications of your genes,
Ready for unraveling,

And the furry beast lay coiled in his maze,
Feasting on the silence of your screams,
The wrinkling skin
That stretched across my bones;
Back before I called your heart my home,
I was (as I lay waiting, waiting, waiting)
alone.

Written 1971.

EVERYTHING LOOKS
BEAUTIFUL
IN THE MORNING

You may pass like the dew
That wakes me on this beach
Beside you,

Where I see by the oval tears
Shining brightly on your
Raven hair

And the sunlight on your rose tattoo –
The morning dew has fallen on
You too.

1977

MY NIGHT WITH CARLA

We were blindfolded by each other,
which made it very hard to drive,
but I simply followed the sound
of the siren in Carla's apartment,
which she set to "high" before
we left, much to the distress
of her neighbors and the terrier
Sam, who lived unbeknownst in
her hamper, addicted to her smell.
(I promised Sam I would never tell
his secret, and I never would, as long
as he didn't blabber about my tail.)

Carla's place always put me in mind
of a one-legged circus clown – I felt like
laughing as soon as I walked in the door,
but I felt like crying too, and sometimes
I did. (That's how I met Sam, as I wept
copious tears while thinking up rhymes
on the crapper, and he couldn't hide
his concern.) Mostly though Carla and I
loved to giggle and guffaw together, and
that's what we did on this night (after
turning off the siren, of course).

                    In fact, we
giggled and guffawed so much this time
that we got kind of sick, then suddenly
we both had to piss. I agreed to let Carla go
first, then smiled at her as I went in the sink.
"I guess this is what love feels like," I intoned,
but my words were drowned out by the sound
of flushing. Sam heard me, though, and he groaned.

Then we traveled on the gondola of our love into
her crimson bedroom, where we made instant love.
Carla punished my lips mercilessly, whipping them
love-brutally while she secreted a silver liquid that
smelled like puppies. (Oh, now I understood Sam!)

I got lost in a fantasy of mating with an antelope,
to the degree that I started making antelope sounds
and trying to climb up her bookcase. (It broke.)
Tired of whipping my lips, Carla became an antelope
too, and we both began braying. Sam couldn't take
anymore, and he charged out of the bathroom, nipping
at our heels. This was just the incentive we needed,
and we made sweet antelope love for hours while
Sam lapped up Carla's silver puddles. I was afraid
for Sam now that Carla had seen him. No more
hiding out in the hamper! But the joke was on me.

When I snapped out of my fantasy, I saw Carla asleep
on the bed, with Sam curled up in her arms. I tried
curling up too, but Sam bared his teeth at me, waking
Carla. "I thought we were friends, Sam," I whined, but
then he pulled down my boxers, revealing my tail.

Carla let out an antelope scream and pointed with her paw
at the door. "Okay," I said, then ran into the bathroom and
tried to hide in the hamper, but the dirty clothes wouldn't
have me. I finally got dressed and took off my blindfold.

I could see clearly now, and it was awful. But
I guess that was life. "So long, Carla," I tossed out, and she
slow-waved at me. I could tell that she felt something too.
Or maybe she was just as sincere as an antelope could be.

1976.

MARIA VICTORIA

Vica I love. Vicky I hate.

The blush of a drawn knifeblade
in the dark
are Vicky's eyes.

Vica's eyes
are still and tell me all,
open like the stars to lovers' eyes.

Vica I love.
The touch of morning stillness
on the sea,
her arm aslant my arm;

swift ocean breezes
rise about her hair,
the body curving
like a coming wave

that breaks upon my lips
to swallow all,
and then withdraws
as with it goes my life.

Vicky I hate!
Vicky I hate!
From a back window
someone hurls a stone:
I know her aim,
the evil of her arm.

No blood can show
How deep a hurt may go.

1972.

HOME

My lover
lies sprawled on the bed,
her body
slashed by the beams
from a streetlamp
her breathing muffled
by a bus's roar –

is this murder mystery scene
really my home?
How did that happen?
How could that be?
Could anyone be happy here?

Why not just turn tail and run
as fast and as far as I can?
Why stick around anymore?

But no, I have to be here because
there's nowhere else for me to be.
I lie down on the bed
and stop breathing.
I listen to my lover's breathing
and try to coordinate
my breathing with hers.
After messing up a few times,
I finally get it right.

Breathing out, breathing in,
gazing at my lover's skin;
breathing in, breathing out,
do away with all that doubt.

Yes, this is my life, where I live.
And "happiness is a choice" –
didn't somebody important say that?
I made certain choices and ended up here.
There has to be a reason for that, right?
I mean, there *were* reasons, I can give
them to you, I can tick them off, one by one

And the end result is, this is my home,
whether I like it or not. So why not like it?
I lean over and try to whisper into her ear,
"I love you." But I can't find my voice.

1978.

GODDESS

U are not yet a memory. U exist in my present mind,
thriving within me on the love and warmth I lavish upon
u. Though u remain somewhere in a distant port yet
unfound in the realm of my travels, I have known u better
in the enlightened moments that we have shared than I
have known anyone else in this vast and busy world.
I shall always think of u as one so close beside me,
even when your path leads apart from mine.
A supreme moment of my existence, and thus of my
time with u, has been the weekend we spent in a
wooden cottage on Fire Island – just the two of us.
While on the ferry rolling towards the misty shore,
we were seized by a compulsion to smile,
for the joy of being together amid the salty waves
was enormous. I seemed to draw strength
from these waves that leapt like dolphins,
as if bringing nature back to the body.

Standing there upon the paint-chipped deck,
soaked with spray in the chilly haze,
I felt pangs of remorse well up inside me,
for the depth of the love I felt for u then
overwhelmed me. I wished these moments
could be immortal, and in my soul they are
preserved as a perfect poem, as a heart-shaped
sound that never ceases.

The cottage stood bold and weatherworn on crystals of
windblown sand. The ocean winds blew with the strength
of countless men, and our dwelling became a fortress, a
monument of personal freedom. We needed no quarrels
to decide the affairs of home, for nature was our judge –
the wisest guide that any man or woman has ever known.
We drifted like two fallen leaves along the ebbing
shoreline, far away from the shadows of our homes.

Gazing into the sunset's crimson eye, I envisioned among the fleecy clouds a shrine sacred amid night's cold ashes, a shrine where loners and lovers who have perceived an uncommon beauty in the dying of the day are conceived newborn with every setting sun.

Suddenly I squeezed your hand with great force – as if u had become nature herself and so would die when the night arrived. U asked me if there was anything wrong, if there were reasons for my sadness. But I could not answer. Once more great throbs of joy overtook my soul, mixed with lonely tears. The mischievous demon of love – who has deceived so many and shall continue doing so until the end of time – sprang from the inner reaches of my heart and strangled the words unuttered within my throat. Then, as my lips met yours, I could see – as if another spirit had risen from the waters and opened my eyes – that u too felt this sadness, overcome with intense emotion. There had been a bond sewn with lasting fibers between our souls, and we were united in a moment of solitude.

Through the blaze of every sunset,
we walk in stillness past the flames.

Upon the black waters we follow a path
as bright as dawn.

Love's demon still plays in passionate fits.

No, u are not yet a memory.

1973.

HOT WATER

I
Couples in the dark
Lie alone together

Two people in the dark
Lie alone together

And listen to the pounding
Of the pipes.

II
No one
pounds the pipes.

The night air is heavy
with the sound of

No one
playing bongos
late at night
or early morning

No one
can be shouted at
"Shut up! There are
people sleeping!"

No one
's life can be taken
into consideration
for the noise.

No one
can be forgiven.

No one
forgives.

III
Couples in the dark
Lie alone together

Two people in the dark
Lie alone together
And dream
of their revenge:

A gun is pointed
at the demon player,
who beats madly on the pipes
for all he's worth –

and then KA-BOOM!!!

His boiling blood is everywhere,
it fills the room.

IV
The rest is silence –
Until the dawn, that is,
when
No one
resurrects
and dreams are ended.

Then the couples
open heavy lids
and, sighing deeply,
drag themselves from bed:

They can feel the blood
start rushing
like hot water
through their veins

While in their heads
It feels like
someone
's beating on a drum.

1980.

NEW

POEMS

I RAN THROUGH THE LAND
OF COLD UNKNOWNS

I ran through the land of cold unknowns
Through Arctic fields of strange indifference
Across a tundra of concealed contempt

I ran through the land of cold unknowns
Slipping on patches of vague hostility,
Slipping and falling into the wet embrace
Of sneering snowdrifts, picking myself up
And falling again through the unseen cracks
In what seemed a shining, undisturbed surface.

I ran through the land of cold unknowns
Burning burning burning
Burning inside
With grand ideas, thoughts and feelings
About the frozen world around me,
Burning with visions of a warmer place
With no icy patches to slip on,
No sneering snowdrifts to fall into,
No unseen cracks to fall through.

I ran through the land of cold unknowns
With a vision of your face in my head,
A vision of your face burning a hole through
The ice crusting over my heart, the icescape
Inside me, unleashing waves of emotion,
A tsunami of pleasure and pain.

I ran through the land of cold unknowns
Through Arctic fields of strange indifference
Across a tundra of concealed contempt
And suddenly you were everywhere,
Everywhere! You had somehow taken over
The world simply by being there.

Then I touched you
And the dead meadows bloomed
Then I touched you
And the tundra turned into a garden
The snowdrifts melted away
And became a flowing dream
Where all manner of living things
Glide through the water,
Where all manner of living things
Fly into the air
And kiss the shocked fishermen,
Who start flying too.

You touched me and
I had no other ideas in my head.
You touched me and
I had no words
Other than what you had said.

You touched me
And I was so glad
That I escaped the tundra,
That I wasn't dead.
But I was suddenly aware
That I wasn't running,
And how had that happened?
A shiver ran through me,
A shiver of fear.

I tried to run but my legs would not move.
A word was projected onto the sky,
But to be honest, I had no idea why.
I just stared up at that word: LOVE.

Oh, it hurt my eyes, like staring at the sun.
My legs got the message. But still I did not run.

YOUR SHOES

Your broken shoes
On the floor of my car
Look so sad, so defeated.

Don't they know
That there is no annihilation
So complete
That it cannot be come back from?

Then again,
Your poor feet, darling, your poor feet
We must have pity on them too.

I kiss your toes, one by one,
Doing my best
To kiss the hurt out of them.

It hurts me to say this, darling,
But maybe we have to consider
That the time has come
To let the defeated
Embrace their defeat,
To let the broken things
Be allowed to stay broken.

Meanwhile, we the undefeated
Will happily walk the extra mile
To find some lovely new shoes
For your lovely old feet.

Or maybe we can accept our love's dare
And simply fly there.

HOUSE WITHOUT DOORS

I loved you. I did.
I think I did anyway.
But the only place
I can remember truly loving you
Is in our House Without Doors.

There was a door – one,
In the front. Otherwise it was
Room after room, everything open.
We always seemed to be in bed
There, in all my memories we are
Making love, with everything
Dream-like, as if we are moving
Together in a painting by Rene
Magritte.

Your brother was in
Another room, making love too.
He was making it with the dark-
Haired ex, not the blonde one.
I think her name was also Rene.

We were unbothered by the sounds
Of their heavy breathing, as they
Were unbothered by ours. It seems
Like nothing bothered us there,
In that house. We floated from
Room to room without a care
In the world. We were young,
Yes, and that was part of it.
But there was something else,
Something special, the air
Had a quality there that it
Had nowhere else. Then again,

Maybe it was just all the weed
That we smoked and all the
Dreams that we dreamed there.

Now that I think of it, your
Brother was renting that house,
He was making his art there.
Caskets with rusty iron nails
On the inside, Barbie dolls
With their throats cut. The
Blood looked so real, I don't
Know how he did that, do you?

He let us stay there, yet in my
Memory, that is our house, a
Place we belonged. I don't
Remember ever belonging anywhere
Else, at least not with you.

Too bad we could never go back there,
That place without doors. I wish
That we could have gone back there.
They tore it down, I believe. Yes,
I'm pretty sure they tore it down.

You were right there. We both were.
After that the world filled up with
Doors, it seemed like there were more
Doors than rooms.

Sometimes it felt like there were
Only doors, and you stopped being
behind any of them a long time ago.

BLOODHOUND

Like a bloodhound
I pick up your scent
As sweet as ripe peaches
In summer, that first juicy bite
With the juice running down
My chin on to my chest hair
But pungent too
Like a thought
That is too large
For the brain to contain.

There is all that and more
When I pull into your space
In your carport, the dank air
Shimmers with the promise of sex.
Upstairs in your place
You're obsessed
With getting everything
Cleaner.
You keep wiping
Everything down,
Then you wipe it again.

"I can't relax
When everything's like this,"
You insist.
And that includes me.
You have me strip naked
And then keep
Wiping me down
Unimpressed
By my erection
Or anything else.

"This isn't sexy,"
I tell you
Which just makes you
Wipe harder
So hard
That my hard-on
Goes away,
As does every desire
Except the one
To leave you, drive away.
Which, very shortly, I do.

Woof.

A SONG OF EXPERIENCE

Yes, you say that age is just a number
(An increasingly large one, I admit)
And that you can rhapsodize about Desire
With the best of the young poets,
But then there comes that moment
When the woman whom you have
Rhapsodized – laid your soul and
The rest of your repertoire bare to –
Excuses herself from the table, and
You are left alone with her friends,
Whose presence you were not happy
About to begin with, though they've
Made it clear that they could not care less.

"Give it up," they say. "Time to accept
That she's never going to sleep with you."
Well, maybe they don't say "sleep with,"
Maybe they say "never going to fuck you"
Or "love you *that* way" or "she don't want
to go near someone's sixty year old cock,"
thereby stripping you of your person-hood.
You're no longer an individual, a distinctive

Human with certain good and bad qualities,
Who may have achieved certain things in his
Life, you have now been reduced to your
Sexual organ, like some boy of fifteen
Who has to jerk off three times a day
To be able to sit in class without squirming,
To be able to hear anything above the
Drumbeat of his own lust. Except that
I'm the teacher now, not the student.

A thought occurs to you of a cycle
That you are part of, a cycle of Desire,
In which you've done your best

To be a person, to flesh out all
The complexities of your character,
But in the end there is only flesh,
In the end all that "fleshing out"
Amounts to nothing compared to
The attraction of pheromones and
Staying a player in the sexual game.
But you push this thought aside, save it
For later when you are writing in your
Journal like a proper old man, and
You press on with your hopeless suit.

"You are making a fool of yourself,"
One of her friends finally says, and
You know that it's true. She should have
Returned from the bathroom by now,
And you suddenly realize that they're all
Just waiting for you to leave so that she
Can come back. You laugh a little –
At yourself or at the situation? – and are
About to stand up when your attention
Is transfixed by the siren scent that the
Woman you desire has left behind.
And so you sit there, suddenly smiling.
(Which freaks everyone out.) And you
Fold your arms and wait. (Which, to your
Great pleasure, freaks them out further.)
Because that's something that old men
Can do very well. We may not be fifteen
Anymore, or even thirty-five, but we've
Had a lifetime of disappointments. So your
Looks of impatience and downright disgust
Will not phase us. We've learned how to wait.

A POEM FOR MY ENEMY

I am fourteen years old and climbing a mountain,
It's a very big mountain, very tall, one of the tallest.

I am in a group of teens, we climb things and
Navigate rivers, we stare into fires and have sex
In the woods. I am one of the youngest in the group
And very aware of it. There's a red-haired girl from Chicago
I am doing my best to impress, but the odds are against me.
We have gone skinny-dipping together and checked each other
Out, She has pale skin like a trout's underbelly, it glowed in the
Moonlight, it shimmered. I want to touch her so badly –
Her newly-formed breasts with their proud little nipples,
The silky-scraggly filaments between her legs –

But it is forbidden; and besides, she has knocked my hand
Away easily, almost carelessly, each time I've tried.
Then one night it rains on an island, all our tents have collapsed
And we're drenched. The girl and I race into the forest,
We are dimly aware of movement around us, things
Undulating in the damp darkness, making strange sounds.
She kisses me full on the mouth, just as she's done many times
In my dreams, but never in life. It's a wet kiss in the rain,
There is water everywhere, but it feels like our element now,
Like we belong here, I want to dive into a rivulet with her
And be swept away. But then a voice in the darkness
Calls out, "Hey, what's going on there? Just stop it!"

That's Jackie, my enemy here. Large-bodied with wire-rim glasses
That often slip down her nose, she is always making fun
Of my scrawny legs, challenging me to bouts of arm-wrestling,
Claiming she could flip me over with one hand and pin me down
With the other. I have no doubt that she could do this and I am
Terrified that she will, or else take me across her knee right
In front of the group. I have almost as many nightmares about this
As I do dreams about the girl from Chicago. And then another
Moment that seems closer to fantasy than anything that could

Really happen, Jackie reaches over and plucks Chicago away
From me, steering her out of the woods. I feel so wet and hungry.

But now we are climbing this mountain, this accumulation of snow and
Ice. Our group is roped together, connected, with Jackie ahead of me
And Chicago behind. "You better keep up!" Jackie warns me. "If I
Feel you dragging me down, I'm gonna kick your butt down the
Mountain." I try to laugh at this, or at least smile, but my lips
Won't form that expression. I look in back of me at Chicago,
But she is laughing and holding hands with another boy,
Her hair looks on fire against the white snow in the morning
Light. Jealousy burns a heart-shaped hole in my chest.

We teenagers carry huge packs on our backs, we move slowly
Like beasts of burden. I glance at our shadows trudging
Beside us, it looks like a race of huge snails making
A pilgrimage to some holy rock, where we will propagate and lay
Our warm eggs, which will pulse in the moonlight like jello.

Two thousand feet short of the summit, Chicago drops out.
"My feet hurt," she whimpers, slipping her shoes off and
Rubbing them. I wish I could rub her feet too, rub them and
Kiss them, but the air is too thin here for fantasies, they flame
Out like flying fish who leap up into the sunshine and never
Come down. Speaking of which – I can hear a soft sound
Rising out of my lungs like a child blowing on a small whistle.
This is my fear, not being able to breathe here. For a moment
I think about dropping out with Chicago, seeing as many of her
Sights as she'll show me, maybe even strolling down her main
Street. But then Jackie levels me with a scornful look, as if
Saying, "Ha! I knew you couldn't do it." I can. I can and I
Will. I may be one of the youngest, but so what? I have what
It takes to get to the top, and I want to see her face when I do.

The sun is up, it is high in the sky like a beating heart,
A heart full of love, but this love is melting the mountain.
The higher we climb the more the mountain is melting
Around us, the path in front of us is slipping away, as are
My chances of reaching the summit. The whistle in my lungs
Has grown into a squeeze box, a squeeze box that is
Squeezing all the air out of me, all the depths of my breath.

I can see the top of the mountain, it is looming above me,
But my breathing is shallow, so shallow, like a big fish
In a small bucket, with just a trickle of water to swim in.
I can see Jackie ahead of me, moving with force and
Determination, but I am so light-headed, so light in my head,
That the flying fish were flying right out of me and taking
Shape in the snow as the girl from Chicago, calling to me
From every snowbank to untie my line and come over and play.

"Hey! Stop pulling on me, you jerk!" Jackie yells at me
Without turning around. This brings me back down to earth,
At least for the moment. "Sorry," I squeak, but I don't
Think she hears me.

"Just five hundred feet to the summit!" someone shouts.

I look up and stumble over my feet and wipe out. My falling
Drags Jackie down too, we both sprawl in the slushy snow,
And the line of climbers stops moving forward. "What the hell?"
Jackie stands up without any help and points down at me.
"Stop leaning on me! I'm not carrying you the rest of the way!"
I nod and try to apologize, but nothing comes out. The climber
Behind me helps me to my feet. "We're almost there," he
Assures me. "Not far to go." I nod, trying to regain my balance,
But Jackie moves furiously upward, and the rope that connects us
Jerks me off my feet and back down to my knees. I stumble forward,
Leaning heavily on my connection to Jackie. I can't breathe now,
Can't breathe at all, my lungs are frozen, and I feel like a puppet
Or a marionette, Jackie's puppet, I keep falling into the slush,

Bouncing up, bouncing along, leaning on Jackie, falling down.
"Stop leaning on me! Stop it! It's not fair!" Jackie cries out,
But she doesn't look around, she keeps going, and she carries me
Over the final ridge and onto a plateau of rock and melted ice.

The summit! We're here!

             The other teens have untied their knots,
They are all seated on the rock formations, conversing, or else
Gazing down at the world, which spreads out beneath us and goes on
Forever. And I'm here too, I've made it all the way to the top,
Even though I couldn't breathe and am still having trouble.
And it's all thanks to you, Jackie. It was all thanks to you. So
Thank you. I couldn't find the words at the time, I was ashamed, and
Besides, I was embarrassed by the squeaky sounds my lungs made.
But you did for me what even the greatest friends I've ever had might
Not have done.

             I wish now that we'd wrestled, it would have
Been an honor to be pinned by you, to be thumped at arm-wrestling.
I hope you've had a good life and that someone somewhere
Did something for you which even a little bit approaches
This huge thing that you did for me, the huge sacrifice you made,
Which I've never forgotten and never will forget, as long
As I'm still on this earth, as long as I'm still breathing.

THOUGHTS DURING ORAL SEX

I suddenly flash on those lovers
In movies of the 1930s, 40s and 50s
Who are burst in on by a
Cadre of cops and newspaper reporters,
And there's always that press
Photographer with the Speed Graphic
Camera whose flashbulb EXPLODES
In the lovers' faces! What if those lovers
Were in the middle of the best sex they
Ever had, maybe they were shy at first,
They couldn't even undress in front of
Each other, but he found out that she
Had a soft spot for peacock feathers,
He bought her a few, and she kissed
Him. Then he got an idea of something
Else he could do with those feathers,
And he whispered it into her ear, and
They were so excited to give it a try
That the clothes just fell off them,
Before they know what is happening
They're entwined like a living organism,
Twisting around, she's never had an orgasm
Before, not a really big one, not the kind of
Orgasm that can change your life – or
At least your perspective. But now she's well
On the way, he's way down inside her,
Deeper than any man has ever gone, she can
Feel a rumble down there, a rumble that
Began as a tickle and then gathered momentum,
It was big and getting bigger, so big that there
Was no way her body could possibly contain
It. She felt herself starting to tremble from her
Toes to her scalp, and she was just about to
EXPLODE when suddenly the door to their
Room flew open, and – Damn! How were they

Always able to get in the front door! I mean,
Didn't anybody use the chain lock? Certainly, by
The 1950s, the news should have trickled down that
Illicit lovers had to take some fucking precautions!
Wake up, lovers, wake up! Just once I'd like to see a
Movie in which the cadre shows up at a particular
"Love nest" or shady hotel room, a key is inserted
Into the door lock and turned – but then, no! The chain
Has been placed in the hook, and no one is getting
In there today! Instead the copulation goes on, and
On and on and on – O guilty pleasure! O forbidden
Ecstasy, uninterrupted! – while outside the cadre is
Bickering, they have never been stymied before and
Frankly don't know how to deal with it. The cop
Makes a snide comment to the detective, who turns
Around and punches him right in the nose. Boom!
Then a fistfight ensues, the blow after blow
Between them mimicking the thrusting that's
Going on inside. The district attorney tries to
Intervene, but both combatants hit him at once –
Boom! He goes down, just as the woman inside is
Gearing up for another crescendo. Then the photo-
Grapher whirls around, he aims his Speed Graphic
Camera at the two fighters and puts his finger on the
Dark button and presses it hard. And everything, inside
And out, slow-motion EXPLODES! Man, I'd go see
That movie. In fact, I might sit through it twice.

THESE THINGS

I.

You absorb
These things
Into your bones.

You feel 20
Or like you remember
How 20 felt
But these things
Oh these things
You've absorbed,
They've absorbed
You
A little bit too.

These things
You've taken
Into
Your body, your mind
Like stray dogs
You have saved
And
Given a home to.

But somehow
All along
They were just
Teaching you
How to be a stray.

II.
These things
You've absorbed
Into your bones
They have also
Absorbed you.

Somehow
These things
Have become
More you
Than you ever were.

Or at least
More you
Than you can ever remember
Being.

THE DANCER

She was a dancer
And she darted into the room
With such a quick step
And now she's dead
Such a quick step
That I didn't see her
Until it was too late
And now she's dead
I was just sitting in the room
Just sitting there reading
An Edgar Allan Poe poem
A Poe poem! A Poe poem!
I can't even remember which one
And she darted into the room
She slipped out of her bathing suit
And was standing there naked
And I was just sitting there
Reading a Poe poem
And now she's dead
Her backside was facing me
She bent over
Drying her private place

What could I say?
She was my sister-in-law
And now she's dead
The words stuck in my throat
I waited for her to turn
To turn around and see me
Oh boy she was gonna kill me
Just kill me
I was gonna be so dead
She would think
I was spying on her
That I came in for that purpose

And was waiting here
I wanted to look away
Really I did
But I have to admit
I was impressed
By the size of her breasts
I hated myself for noticing
But what a shapely behind
I didn't expect that
What a really shapely behind
I guess because she was a dancer

And now she's dead
She turned to the side
Now I had a full view
A full view of the panoply
Of her completeness
Oh this is bad
Oh this is so bad
I have to do something
She's going to see me
How has she not seen me
And now she's dead
She had a piece of white
Lint stuck in her pubic hair
A piece of lint or was it a thread
Either way I was a dead man
Watching her pick it out of her pubes
And now she's dead
I don't think she liked me
Even before this
I'm pretty sure she never liked me
And that was for no real reason
That was just for me being me
Now this was going to give her
Such a big reason to hate me

To hate me and never forgive me
So what could I say to make it better
At this point I could just make it worse
By saying anything, there really was
No explaining my presence away
And now she's dead
Oh no, now she's bending over again
Now she's drying her feet and ankles
Why is this happening?
Can this get any worse?
Oh yes it can
Because I'm getting a hard-on
And now she's dead
I really have to take up dancing
God knows I need to take up dancing
Would a compliment do any good
If I say something nice
About her breasts and her backside
No no! that would just make it worse
But how could anything else
Make it worse than it already was
Oh I was such a dead man
She died in a hospital bed
She shrank down to seventy pounds
I wanted to say goodbye
But her sister would not let me see her
Apparently she didn't want to be seen
She never saw me that day
I saw her but somehow
She didn't see me
Sitting there with a book
Of Edgar Allan Poe poems
Over my terrified hard-on
And I never told anyone
But I'm telling you now
I saw the panoply of her completeness

And she was beautiful
An elegant dancer
She moved quickly
But not quick enough
None of us is quick enough
I will never forget her
It's true
That will always be with me
Her darting into the room
With such a quick step
The step of a dancer
And I will never forget

THE COMPLAINT

When I could have said no to you
I didn't
When I could have turned my back on you
I didn't

But you had no problem
Turning your back on me
You went out of your way
To try to destroy me

In the end all I got from you
Was your silence
In the end all I got from you
Was never having to hear you again

This may in its way have been
The best gift I've ever been given.
This may in its way have actually
Saved my life.

So that complaint I had
About your being unkind?
Yeah, well, never mind.

THE PANDA

For Yingying

She missed the bus.
"He had no remorse,"
Her father said.

She missed the bus.
Her boyfriend couldn't
Understand. What kind
Of country is this?

She missed the bus.
There was no reason for it.
He was smart, with a
Masters in Physics.

She missed the bus.
Her mother stood on
Her dead daughter's
Balcony and cried.

She missed the bus.
It was not in his nature
To hurt anyone, his father
Insisted.

She missed the bus.
"It was supernatural,
How hard she fought me,"
he told his girlfriend.

She missed the bus.
"Everything will turn out
All right," he told his
Mother from jail.

She missed the bus.
He tossed her out
In three separate
Garbage bags.

She missed the bus.
His girlfriend gave him
Up. He refused to look
In her eyes at the trial.

She missed the bus.
She was already late
For her appointment.

She missed the bus.
He pulled up in his car.
He had a trustworthy face.

She missed the bus.
He laughed when she told him
Her name.

"That sounds like the
Name of a panda," he said.
"Not the name of a person.
A real human being."

ADAM AND EVE: A CLOSER LOOK

Adam, we are told, is created
First. The crowning achievement
Of the Almighty, that classic
Over-achiever. Intended to
Take dominion over the Fruit
Of the earth and the Beasts
Of the field. Okay, check.

But then Adam becomes
Lonely – what? Why? How
Does he even know what "Lonely" Is?
Does he see the animals mating
And that puts an idea in his head?
Or do animals not have sex yet,
Since life is still lived in Innocence?
But no, the animals have to have sex,
That's what animals do, but maybe it's not
Considered sinful yet? (How could animal sex
Ever be seen as sinful? That makes no sense.)

Anyway God (we are told)
Creates Eve from Adam's rib,
Which raises so many questions –
Like how does Adam have a rib
To spare? Was he born that way,
Or does the Creator just whip up
An extra rib out of thin air? And why
Take a piece of Adam to build her
From? Why not create her
Independently, the way Adam was?

(Still wondering about Adam's
"Loneliness," which just doesn't
Add up. I mean, Time as we know it
Didn't exist yet, so how could it hang

Heavy on Adam's shoulders? Nothing
Ever changed, because every day
Was exactly the same. So what was it
That Adam was yearning for? Not that
The idea of "yearning" really makes any
Sense either, at least not for Adam.)

But no, I guess the point of this Bible story
Is that she's not independent, Eve is created

To be Adam's Companion, his celestial fuck buddy,
Connected to him from her Core. Wow, Adam,
Good luck with that. Just try having that therapy
Session, bro. I guarantee you end up in knots.

I mean, do they start out loving each other?
Or is it unequal right from the get-go?
Does Adam have any feeling for her at all?
Do they have sex right away or is it not really
An issue, they just start screwing like dogs
(who didn't exist yet)? Not really clear.

And then there's The Snake. I mean, come on!
How is Eve supposed to deal with something
Like that? I mean, folks, it's a setup, a
Classic setup, like a Mafia hit! She's not just
Created to trust, you could say that she's created
From trust! Her flesh, her blood, her bones –
Including that rib – I mean, what could be a
Bigger symbol of trust than that rib, yanked
Right out of Adam's skeleton, a
Fundamental piece of his structure!

And how could a living being – man or
Woman or elephant, who could be painted
In a mural as an allegorical figure of Trust –
How could this being be blamed for being

Fooled by a snake, who would be painted
In that same mural as representing Deceit,
Pure Deception? I mean, Eve is naked! By
Which I mean not just without clothes but
Without any way to defend herself. Without
Suspicion! She has no suspicion because that's
How she was created! And without suspicion
What chance does she really have? I mean, please.

One thing we are told that Eve has is curiosity.
She is curious, but Adam isn't. So Adam and Eve
Are told not to eat from the tree of knowledge, and
Adam says, got it. Message received. Because, let's
Face it, Adam is a company man, he has no capacity
For independent thought and will always do just
What he's told to. And we're supposed to
Admire him for that? For being God's Golem?

So in that allegorical mural we spoke of before,
Adam would be the figure of Obedience. He will
Always do as he's told because that's how he was made,
To follow orders. But how could he really appreciate Eve,
Much less love her, if she has the attribute of curiosity,
While he doesn't? He looks at the world and sees black
And white, while she sees all these shades of gray, all this
Nuance and texture. And whose fault is that? Who
Created her that way? Who? Was this just a big joke then,
A big cosmic joke, taking Adam's rib and then shaping
This woman around it who has a gift of perception
That Adam doesn't? Of course she responds to the
Snake's "subtlety" – as it is called – because she has
Been created with subtlety too. And of course she responds
To temptation, because she is open to such things, she has
That quality, while Adam doesn't. So how can we admire
Adam for resisting temptation when he cannot be tempted?
And how can we blame Eve? She is susceptible. So what?

All kidding aside now (sort of), I know that the issue on the divine
Table is one of Free Will. "Eve made a choice and now the rest of us
Have to live with the consequences." Blah blah blah. That sounds like
Adam talking, don't you think? Or the Supreme Leader speaking
Through him. Because what good is Salvation if it consists in simply
Following orders, doing what you are told? And how is Free Will
A part of that equation? Eve questions everything, Adam questions
Nothing, what kind of pairing is that, God? I mean, what did the Big U
Have on Your Big Nosey Mind? Adam is a cipher, he wouldn't know
About Free Will if it gave him a blow job at high noon (again, Time
Not being a thing yet back then, probably blow jobs not either).

No, Eve is the one who can choose, and she chose. But she didn't
Choose a snake or a worm-riddled apple over Adam. Eve chose
Anything but Adam. Anything. Because anything had to be better
Than being a person with choice who has had none. And even though
You will see tragedy in her eyes when she turns around, still chewing
That sour apple, a moment later – after a Big Pin has been stuck
In their Divine Bubble, and wrist-watches rain down from the sky –
You can spot a small but telling smile on Eve's face, as she and Adam
Are kicked out of the Paradise that never was a paradise for her.

And if you listen hard enough, you can almost hear her voice
As she turns to Adam and mutters under her breath,
"So you think you were lonely before…?"

POOR SALOME

oh Salome, poor Salome,
excuse me if I still hold a grudge
for all the effort
you put into that dance

the shimmy and the shaking
the crying and the faking
in front of that judge
every time I think about
the dotted line
I had to sign on
the dotted line
you drew on my neck
with the knife that
your lawyer gave you
your lawyer gave you
the ideas, what to say
but you gave the performance
the best one of your career
you were the dancer and the dance
you were the dancer of the year
and the judge was your biggest supporter
she gave you a standing O
and brought out the silver platter
she shined it right in my face
she made me a part of the show
when all that should have mattered
was to preserve the love we once had
was to separate the good from the bad

oh Salome, poor Salome,
when I wiped away all the tears
and looked up from the chopping block
I was thinking about all the years
and our hundreds of thousands of fucks
and now it came down to this case

in case you don't know
what happened there really sucks
even more than your dance did
I was willing to give you a lot
but not
that final gift of my head
I walked out with it held high
remembering what we once said
about always staying true
to the world of me and you
we didn't even say goodbye
It's true I made mistakes
It's true we grew apart
But there was still a lot of love left
now I regret it all
from when we met, right from the start
and no matter how many showers I take
I cannot completely get rid of
that dotted line you drew
or the memory of you
dancing in court like a snake

oh Salome, poor Salome
Now there's nothing more to say
all the words already said
I have everything that matters
you have an empty silver platter
soon the knots will be untied
while I'm still alive inside
I am thankful every day
to be rid of you, your memory
while you, poor Salome,
have already had your big chance
you live in the empty palace of you and me
while freedom is my happy dance
and what will be will be.

THE STRIPPER

The stripper looked like
Somebody famous,
But I couldn't think who.
Marlene Dietrich? Madonna?
Someone like that.
She was naked, writhing onstage,
A Mayan Salome,
And every man in the place
Wanted to put his head on her platter.
What was she doing here anyway?
She was high-class, a Sex Goddess,
This place was a dump.
The very idea of A.C. was a joke,
There was a fan in the back
That only blew the hot air around.
Her brown skin was sweating,
Little rivulets rolled down her body
Like tears, like her flesh was weeping,
While on her face she wore
The mask of a sensual smile
That was intended for everyone here
And for no one. You could have her
For a small price.
You could never possess her.

Later she came to my table
And put one hand
Lightly on my crotch
While with the other
She touched my fingers.
"You buy me a drink?"
She said in English.
I did. I could feel
The heat under the table
From her private part

Which was so public.
Her sweat smelled like sex.

At a nearby table
I could see the fat guy
With the short hair
In his Navy whites
As he mimed putting
A dick in his mouth
And swallowing cum.
He nodded encouragingly.

I touched
The stripper's breast,
It was hard as a callous,
Like something
That has been bruised
So many times
That it's turned
Permanently hard
Like a shell or like
A shield against further sorrow.
Touching it now
Was like entering
Stephen King's Dead Zone,
Except what I saw there
Was not her pain
But my own:

The end of my marriage,
The nasty breakup,
The pile of lawyer's bills,
The grotesque scenes in court.
Then coming out here to Tijuana,
Walking through the worst part of town,

Daring anyone to come at me.
Strolling over to join a crowd
Of men watching two dogs fuck
In the middle of the dusty street.
Smiling along with everyone else
When the bitch began
Moaning in her high-pitch.

And where would I go
After this? To buy drugs
And then drive to the border.
Not because I wanted to sell
The drugs or even enjoy them
Myself. Just because I wanted
To see what would happen,
If the guards would stop me
Or not, if they would bust me.
But I couldn't see that far ahead,
So I guess I'd find out.

I took my hand
Off the stripper's breast
And kissed her right on the mouth,

The way I kissed my wife
When I was in love with her.
The stripper's eyes
Widened in shock,
There was an audible gasp
In the dark club,
A stirring of outrage,
I could see the two bouncers
Coming straight for me,
One from each side.
I took out my wallet
And tossed two Andrew Jacksons
On the slick-with-sweat table

And then walked outside
Where I was struck
By a blast of hot air
That seemed to come
From a furnace.

Now where were those drugs?

GHOST GIRL

Who were you, who burst into my bedroom
At 4 AM, flinging the white door wide open?

I was sleeping alone, the woman I loved had
Recently left me, taking our 5 year old daughter
To her new home. It was a hard time for me, I
Wasn't sleeping well, and yes, it's true that I was
Waking up often, but the last thing I ever expected
To see when I did was a 10 year old girl with thick
Blond hair past her shoulders, wearing a white nighty
Under a light-blue, knee-length robe cinched at the
Waist, and holding a very large brown teddy bear in
Her arms. She looked a lot like Pippi Longstocking
In the books that my little girl loved, though I think
Pippi's hair is red. I had read her those books many
Times before naps, but now here this girl was, waking
Me out of a dream that faded fast, almost as fast
As she moved through the room to the open door
Of my clothes closet. "Who are you? What do you
Want?" I asked her breathlessly. She didn't turn
Around or respond in any way to my questions.

The sound of my voice in that empty room
In the middle of the night scared me. It meant
That this was really happening, it wasn't just
All in my head. But then the next moment
Something happened that blew away any firm
Notion of what was real and what wasn't.

She stood in front of the empty half of the
Closet, the half where the clothes of the woman
Who left me once hung. Then there was a
Movement in the solid wall, a streak of light
Opened up there, then a long hallway, which
She began walking down. I saw her walk

Through the wall and down this corridor,
I heard footsteps as she kept walking, I
Watched her get smaller and smaller until
She became just a small dot in the distance.
Then the hallway itself disappeared. I got out
Of bed, walked to the wall, but it was as solid
As ever, with no sign of what she just did.

So who are you, ghost girl, and why were you
There? Do you have a destiny that has nothing
To do with me? Or did you just want to add
Your mystery to all the other ones haunting my
Days and nights back in that ghost-ridden time?

PALINDROME DREAM

I wake up on 02/22/20 – Palindrome Day,
At least by the American calendar –
With a dream still swirling around in my
Brain: I'm forty years old, and a dark-haired
Jewish woman of the same age begs me
To help her get pregnant, saying her life
Will have no meaning without a child.
She brings me to a sacred shrine,
a large dark room in a synagogue,
Where a number of her eggs have been
Extracted and placed in petri dishes, with
A burning candle beside each one. There
Is a holy hush in the air as I take out my
Equipment and get it in gear. Then I fire
Off shot after shot of thick white liquid –
Bing! Pow! Splat! – massive laser shots,
All in the direction of the burning candles.
Most of them go awry, but one moonshot
Bounces off a post, skids along a wall and
Lands in a petri dish, right on top of her egg.
The woman calls me over, we stand there
Watching them fertilize. The woman puts
A top on the dish, she takes it away with her.
Nine months later our bouncing baby boy is
Born. His name is Abba (a palindrome –
of course!). It is a dream come true for both
Of us! And now our lives are full, they have
A meaning that they didn't before. And while
I don't recall how everything worked out
Between the woman, the baby and me, I
Feel sure it was all good. Because that's why
Palindrome days are so rare, coming only
Once or twice a year at most. They are the
Calendar kidding us, like the little white lie
That a friend might tell to make you feel happy.

3:45 AM WOMAN

Sleeping with you was like
Sleeping with an Edgar Allen Poe story

I know that sounds cruel
But I don't mean it cruelly.
You drew me in, I was completely
Entranced, and I wanted to know more.
Then there was a hook and a twist
and in the end there was horror.

Sleeping with you was like
Sleeping with an Edgar Allen Poe story

Somehow it was always 3:45 AM
Always 3:45 AM with you
We were always awake then
Always in the middle of something
Horrible, something scary and weird

You were haunted by the death
of your mother, haunted
that you weren't there when she died.
You had spent night and day
in the hospital with her,
night and day, day and night.
You were there to make sure
she got the best care
and nothing terrible happened
but then the moment you left
something terrible happened
the very thing you were there
to prevent. But you didn't.

Her dying word was your name
Her dying word was your shame
The nurse had to tell you about it

You hated that nurse, didn't trust her.
You were sure your mother's death
was her fault, but it was too late now.
Too late to accuse her of anything
Too late to point your finger at anyone
else. It was too late for anything now.
You left the room, your mother was dead.
You came back, she was cold in the bed.
It was your fault, your inner voice said.

She died at 3:45 AM
but she was not dead for you

she was living on in your head
she was screaming mad in your head
where she was dying over and over
and each time you weren't there
and each time she called you a liar
and each time your hair was on fire

Sleeping with you was like
Sleeping with an Edgar Allen Poe story

Where it was always 3:45 AM
and you were too tortured to sleep
I finally had to close the book on you
Sorry, I thought I could help you
But horror's not really my thing.
Or maybe it is in a way, though
only at 3:45 AM, when I can hear you
in my head, pleading and screaming.

WAKING UP IN JOANNA'S POEM

I woke up at 3 AM with a memory
In my mind, nagging at me. I was
Supposed to do something that I
Hadn't done. What? Buy a book?
Yes, right. But what book? And why
Was it so pressing that it woke me up in the
Middle of the night? My friend Joanna –
It had something to do with her. We had just
Met at a conference in Boston –
Had she told me about a book there? Damn,
Why couldn't I remember? I took out my
Phone, wrote Joanna an email, then back to slumber
Land. When I woke up again, there was this:

> We were on a train in Boston
> I remember running to catch it
> We weren't paying attention to the time
> and there I was, dragging my suitcase
> and trying not to spill my coffee
> and not understanding the whole deal
> about trains being rerouted that day
> and then seeing that tall, scholarly-
> looking gentleman with the long white
> beard wearing a beautiful keepah and
> being a little transfixed because he
> reminded me of Rabbi Shay Mintz
> from Buffalo who had recently passed away.
> I'd had a particular fondness for Rabbi Mintz
> because he had been very kind to me
> when I first moved to Buffalo and
> always remembered me even though
> I rarely attended services and
> because he and his beautiful wife Lila
> were often seen walking on busy highways
> to get to services on Shabbat.

The scholarly man with the white beard
came over to us on the train and told us his
story about Halina Nelkin, who as a young girl
had survived Auschwitz and Ravensbruck and
six other camps. Somehow she was able to keep
a diary about what she went through, and somehow
she was able to smuggle it out and get it published.
And he knew Halina, had known her, had been her friend;
she lived in Brookline until 2009, and he had just
come from a memorial for her. I felt a little bit blessed
by his choosing to tell us. Then we hopped off the train
because of all that crazy rerouting, and after waiting for

a bus that didn't seem like it would ever come (and
never did), I started to panic about missing my flight,
called for an Uber, who got us to the airport in record time,
although how would I know it was record time when I
know nothing about Boston traffic patterns or infrastructure?
But I do remember rushing into the airport, going
through the security line with my suitcase, leaving
the line to take my suitcase back to the check in,
running back to meet you in line, meeting a photographer
with long hair who looked familiar or who knew you (or
thought he did) and then making it to my departure gate
on time. And then you headed off to your gate and I
ordered Halina's book on Amazon and flew home.

Oh yeah, Halina's book! Her diary. Auschwitz.
How could I have forgotten that? What a great memory
You have, Joanna! What a great memory.

PRAYER TO MY DAUGHTER

This is the love that hurts the most
This is the love that gives the most
This is the love that changed my heart
This is the love I can't live without

When your mother left me
When she bought a home
That I couldn't even pay for
in my dreams
in my dreams
the angel whispered your name
before you had a name
before you had a form
you had a form for me
you had a form and a place
the angel whispered into my inner ear
in my heart was your face
so full of joy, wonder and
your room was so empty
when you weren't there
when you weren't there
it was hard for me to go

near it, I couldn't
protect you, I couldn't
see you at so many birthdays
with cake and ice cream
that melts in the sun
I felt like ice cream
when re-frozen, it looks just fine
but something feels wrong
when you chose to live full-time
with your mom, I melted inside

I love you whatever you do
I've found a new shape, I'm happy
to give you a ride whenever you
need one, you make the world
livable, a place where I'm happy
to be, I'm happy to be anywhere
near you, I'm happy to be anywhere
in a world that contains you
never feel constrained by anything
or anyone who wants you to be
other than the best version of you
just do what you need to do

I will be there applauding
you give me reason to get up in the morning
never question my love, that's the thing
I meant to tell you, I meant to say
sun streams into your room now
as it did on the day
we brought you back here
where there's nothing to fear
and I sat in the gliding chair
for as long as you needed me to
to feel safe and nod off
I will always be in that chair for you
just one thing I ask
please don't die
before me, whatever you do
that would be more than I could bear
more than I could take
it would be poison tears
on the ice cream and cake
you have to live for years
beyond me, or my life melts to
nothing, or my life disappears
this is my prayer to you, honeypie
this is my prayer

THE TALE OF THE VIOLIN GIRL

I was in my life, I was in my busy life,
Earning some side money as a theater
Critic (not in my original plans, but plans
Change, as do expectations), and I was running
Late for a show's curtain time, and I was running
Down the stairs of a parking garage, running
As fast as I could. I kept running down stairs,
Staircase after staircase, then I came to another
Door, burst through it, and I came to a final door,
That surely would let me out on the street – but
No. This last door was locked. And I turned
Around just as the door behind me slammed
Shut. And locked automatically. And I found
Myself in a 10 foot by 12 foot cell that smelled
Like piss. "Help! Help! Help!" I screamed,
Then waited for a response, for the voice
Of a garage attendant or even a stranger.
But there was nothing. Nothing. "Help!"

Above me were the gray metal stairs
That I had just been running down before
I ended up here. Surely someone else
Would be coming down those stairs any
Moment. Surely someone would spare me
The need to take out my phone and let the
World know that I am trapped in this
Piss prison. But no. No one came. And I
Didn't hear the sound of anyone coming.
And it was 7:58, the play (about a young
Woman trying to break away from her family
And face the world on her own) would be
Starting in just a few minutes. I took out
My phone and made calls, I screamed out
Over and over, but nobody came. No other

Cars drove by. No other people walked down
The stairs. The minutes kept ticking past. And
I felt so completely alone. So absolutely alone.

Just when I had called the garage for the third time
And was reduced to rattling the metal door to the
Parking area – feeling still like this couldn't be real,
And was I a character in a hip novel, one of those
Sleek Indie derivatives of Camus' The Stranger –
then I heard someone's footsteps coming down the
Stairs. "Hello?" I called out. "I'm down here. I'm
Trapped." The steps stopped right above me. Then
They continued on slowly. The person came into view:
A dark-haired woman in a denim dress carrying a

Violin case. I saw her looking around for the source
Of the sounds she'd been hearing. I'm suddenly
Aware of how weird this will look from the outside,
How weird and creepy. A guy in a cage under the
Stairs. Yeah, that's just how I want to be seen.

"Hey there. Hello? Down here," I piped up, in as
Engaging and upbeat a voice as I could muster
Under the circumstances. She was standing on the
Second floor landing now and looked down in my
Direction. "Hi, I'm trapped in here. Could you let
Me out?" I smiled, shrugging my shoulders. "What?"
She asked, blinking, trying to focus. I told her the
Tragic tale of how I had come to be locked up here,
And, frankly, it sounded suspicious even to me, as if
I was recounting a fairy tale, in which she was the
Princess and I was the frog. Oh, but I'm really a
Prince, you see, you just have to kiss me to find out.
That is, you need to trust me. Just because I'm in a
Piss-soaked cage doesn't mean I'm not a good person.

As she stood there thinking over whether or not to
Open the door, she could very well have been the

Girl of my dreams. Slender, medium height, with
Warm brown eyes full of a mix of good humor and
Wariness, she looked around for a garage attendant
Or anyone else who could back her up. But of
Course there was no one. "So that door doesn't
Lead to the street?" she asked. I shook my head.
"Wow, that's really dangerous. There's not even
A warning sign." I nodded, adding that I was
Already late for a play I was supposed to review.
"What a mistake," I thought, as soon as the
Words were out of my mouth. Everybody hates
Critics. Now she'll never open the door.

She took a few steps in my direction and I
Expected her to walk right past, to walk away.
Instead she pushed open the door, and I stepped
Out of my cell and was free. Free! I took a big
Breath of freedom (still urine-scented) and smiled
My thanks to the Violin Girl, who nodded curtly
Back at me. The fairy tale ending, of course, would
Have us walk off together, hand in hand, into a world
Of living happily ever after; and we did walk down
The sloping ramp side by side, towards the parking
Garage exit. But then she veered off to the
Left, and my life as a critic, my critical life,
Took me off to the right. "Thanks!" I called
After her, and she nodded without looking
Around, the violin case swinging back and forth
In her hand. This seemed like the wrong
Ending, so wrong, and as I sit here now in my
Lockdown, self-isolated in a darkening room
In a city where I did not grow up, I long for a

New resolution, one in which the Hand of Fate
Gives a stronger push, shoving the two of us
Together in a way that no reality (regardless
Of pathogens!) can put asunder. And where
The two of us dance to the rhythms of her violin
Music, her bow skimming over the taut strings
Like a shiny flat stone over the bright surface
Of dark and mysterious waters.

THE ADULTERERS

— I saw someone on the street
  Last night who looked just like you.
  Just like you. It was uncanny.

— Really? Wow. Where was this?

— Downtown. In our old haunts.

— Did you say hello to this person?

— I was going to.

— What happened?

— I saw that it wasn't you.

— What gave me away?

— Well, I smiled but you just kept on
  Walking. It felt like you were
  Walking right out of my life.

— Except that it wasn't really me,
  Remember?

— How could I forget? Still,
  It was so uncanny.

— Stop using that word. I hate you
  When you use words like that.
  That's what makes me want to
  Leave you.

— Oh, so you do want to leave me?

— When you use words like that, yes.

— Well, not if I leave you first.

— What?

— Nothing.

— I've heard enough of this shit.
  I'm gonna go take a walk.

— Me too. Maybe I'll see you out there.
  On the street. Walking.

— Just don't say anything if you do.
  Just walk right by me.

— As if you were someone else?

— That's right. As if you never saw me
  Before and didn't have a clue.

— I'll try to remember that.

— Do.

WHEN IT DID HAPPEN

When it did happen
it was not at all what I imagined
As soon as you took your clothes off
I could tell that something was off
Your face and body did not go together
Your face said one thing and your body another
Your face was painted by Andrew Wyeth
while your body was from Picasso's Blue Period
It wasn't soft and curvy at all
It had hard edges, right angles
Your breasts were large yet somehow sorrowful
Your body was filled with anguish and torment
You smiled at me with kindness
but your body couldn't respond to my touch
It was like stroking granite.

Your vagina seemed embarrassed
about how open it was, how accessible
It seemed to yearn for something to hide behind
But, alas, there was nothing
I entered you but I never felt inside
Never felt anything changing
You seemed to get further and further away

Like we were fucking in different rooms
In a film where everything was out of sync
where the mouths moved and there was no sound
where the silences were filled with people talking

I knew you less after that night
than I had that first moment
when we smiled at each other
from across the room at the party,
when you seemed like a person
I needed to get to know better
and you appeared
To want to get to know me.

THE WEDDING OF FACT AND FICTION

I.

You know this is a mistake
The moment you walk in the door
With your new girlfriend Cassie
And her six year old daughter, Giselle.
First off, Giselle has a real phobia
When it comes to dogs, and there are
Thirty of them in the room. Literally
Thirty dogs (yes, you've counted), it seems
That every guest except you has brought one.
Is this a wedding of people or canines?

"Did you do this on purpose?" Cassie
Screams at you above the screams of her
Daughter, as guests begin (very reluctantly)
To herd the dogs into another room.
You're here because of the groom,
He's an actor-turned-IRS agent who
Doesn't have many friends (you're one
Of two, the other's a deaf accountant).
He made you promise that you would show.
His bride is gorgeous – I mean, spectacular –
Long raven tresses, slim waist and breasts
That her low-cut gown reveals
Are remarkably perky. (Hey,
You're sitting across from her,
You can't help but see.) "I was
A corporate attorney in Buenos Aires,"
She says, "but I came here to be
An actress." What kind of actress
You wonder, when she confides that
She's not wearing panties, then brushes
Her skirt aside to give you a peek.

Just then Cassie comes back with Giselle,
They both have red eyes and look like
They've been weeping. "What are you crying
About?" you ask Cassie. "Life is so hard,"
She says. "So much is promised, so little
Delivered. And love dies." Uh-huh. Not
The first time you've heard this. You keep
Trying to break up with her, but she plays
The squeezebox so well. She whips it out
Whenever your tone gets too serious,
And then, no matter what else has been
Going on, you can't keep from dancing.

II.
Giselle blurts out, "I'm thirsty!" So we go
In search of orange soda. Imagine our surprise
When we come upon an orange Labradoodle
Who has tipped over the only bottle and is
Lapping it up. "Go away! Shoo!" you yell,
And the Labradoodle snarls, causing Giselle
To grab her forehead and pace the room,
Shaking her head. "Oh my God, she looks
Just like Eleanora Duse in Ibsen's Ghosts,"
A thin man remarks. "Yes, that's one
Of her favorite videos," Cassie tells him.
As they smile at each other for a little too
long and Giselle hams it up, the Labradoodle
Sneaks away with the soda. You pour
A glass of Tropical Punch for Giselle, who
Immediately tosses it right in your face.
"Oh my God, that's just like Liz Taylor in
Who's Afraid of Virginia Woolf?" the thin man
Says again, and Cassie remarks, "Yes, that's
Her all-time favorite!" Then they nod at each other
For so long that you get really jealous. So jealous,
In fact, that you give thanks for not bringing a gun.

III

Just then there is screaming from
The other room that is even louder
Than the screaming in this one. You turn
To run there along with everyone else
When Cassie grabs your arm so hard
That you can hear the bones crack.

"Don't go. Please. There's no way
That's going to be as exciting as it
Sounds," she whispers, even though
No one else is listening. "It's just
Going to be another disappointment,
And I can't take that. I can't take any more
Let-downs. Life is just a series of bouncing
From one bummer to the next. Don't look
At me that way, you know it's true. I thought
You were going to be different, you promised
So much, in my head I was already directing
The documentary about our brilliant lives,
The way that we re-defined our era, the way
We both typified our times and vaulted beyond
Them. There was no limitation on who we could
Be, on what we could become, but then we went
To bed together, and it all came crashing
Back down to earth.... Missionary? Really?
And I was praying that you would be impotent
Like a real poet, with a soft white worm that
Would just lie there like a dying thing, so I could
Breathe life back into it, so I could spend years
Of our precious time together nursing you back to
Health, like in an early Hemingway novel. But no, you
Were hard as a truck driver, which just broke my heart.

"There would be no new mythology. There would
Be no ground-breaking documentaries or
Re-definition of what it means to be human.
No one would study our love as a way to
Understand what it meant to be alive in this time
And place, we would not be Scott and Zelda, Nick
And Nora, or even Masters and Johnson.
We would not be avatars of our age
For the future. I had to lower my
Expectations so far that I felt like I
Was living in the downstairs apartment.
And you know very well, we couldn't afford
That apartment. But what choice do we have?
It's better than living out on the street."

Giselle made a weird, sub-human sound,
Then she threw up on the floor in three
Brightly-colored puddles. "Oh my God,
Just like Linda Blair in The Exorcist!"
The thin man puts in. Everyone ignores him.
You know in your heart that you have to break
Up with this woman. But where are the words?

IV
Oh boy. The need to get away from that vomit
Is pressing, what the hell has she eaten? You search
your mind for some memory of lunch, but it seems to
Have taken place on another planet, in a galaxy
Far, far away. Cassie inventively sweeps the
Puddles into a plastic container with a plastic
Ladle, leaving three brightly-colored circles
On the floor that seem to mean something, like
An ancient symbol for the mystery of life, or a
Dire warning about a dangerous infection that
Threatens the world. Or maybe it's just a stain.

"Where's Giselle?" Cassie asks, searching around.
I shrug my shoulders, a gesture that Cassie hates.
("It makes you look like that character out of a
Bugs Bunny cartoon. Elmer what's-his-name."
"Fudd," I always remind her, but not this time,
As she's already on her way into the other room.)

V

Giselle stands with the thin man on the edge of
The crowd, gesticulating wildly as if having an
Attack of some kind. Cassie sweeps her up
Into her arms and glares at the thin man. "She
Does a great Katherine Hepburn," he whines.
The next thing you're aware of are the exiled dogs
Scratching on the doors and the walls, whining
Plaintively to be allowed back. Their cries sound
Almost like words, almost like warnings about
What we are liable to do without their influence,
Without the controls they exert on our behavior,
Without the leashes they put on our madness.
"That's going a little too far, don't you think?"
You would like to tell them, but you know
They already don't have the highest opinion
Of you, and besides, there are those teeth.

In the room, a violent argument is taking place
Between the groom and his other friend besides
You, Felix the deaf accountant. They are shouting
Numbers at each other, increasingly large numbers,
Which is all you can understand beyond their
Belligerent tone. "He's accusing Felix of coming
On to the Bride," Cassie tells you, as if translating
From a foreign language. The Bride seems transformed,
Transfigured, her face reminds you of martyrs, of

Saints, from the paintings of Fra Filippo Lippi, who
Was of course a noted defiler. A sound issues from
The Bride's mouth, a high-pitched sound, that
Brings to mind a gaggle of castratos singing
A Gregorian chant. This mixes uneasily in the
Air with the angry shouting of the two men, it
Feels like two abstract armies are battling there.
"Disappointed?" you ask Cassie. "Always," she
Murmurs. "Extremely. It's really almost unbearable."
She has such a cute look on her face when she says
This, it reminds you of Audrey Hepburn in *Breakfast
At Tiffany's*, except without the breakfast.
This reminds you of how hungry you are,
You haven't had breakfast either, and lunch –
Ah lunch! It is lost in a miasma of memories,
Floating somewhere in the darkness of Space,
You imagine yourself as an astronaut leaving
The Mothership, but bound to it by life-giving
Cables, as you go in pursuit of your lunch, or
At least the memory of it. You are getting
Closer and closer, it shines against the blackness
Of Space like the Holy Grail in a Wasteland.
But just as you are about to put your dirty mitts
On it and haul it in, just as you are about to
Score what feels like a victory for Mankind
(And Womankind too), just as you are about to
Become the hero of the legend in your own
Mind – the air in the room explodes with music!

Yes, it's true. Cassie has brought out her squeeze-
Box and is playing a polka. Giselle looks upset,
She is shaking her head back and forth with such
Force, you're afraid that she'll hurt herself. The
Room itself feels like a skeptic sniffing its nose,
Unsure if it likes some new smell and inclined to
Reject it. This only causes Cassie to squeeze her

Box more intensely, she has a desperate look on
Her face. You don't know about the room, but
Your own feet want to dance, though you do
Your best to restrain them. The hands of Felix
The accountant start speaking sign language
In time to the music, you don't know what he's
Saying but you can tell that it's good. Then the
Bride stands up and starts dancing! She's dancing
Right toward the Groom. You look at the Groom
And do a double-take! He seems to have shed a
Skin, removed a mask, you can see your friend
Again, that happy-go-lucky actor who did a
One-man version of *War and Peace* and
Brought down the house. You feel so happy
To see him again that your feet begin
Dancing in His direction with your arms
Open. The Groom turns toward you and
Smiles, you can see that he's dancing too,
And in that moment you rejoice that you
Came to his wedding, it has all been worth it!
Just then the thin man knocks you out
Of the way so that the Bride and Groom
Can dance with each other. They love
Each other, they do! You can see it right
There in their eyes, and in their feet,
The way they're moving in sync with
Each other. You look around, and –
Everyone's dancing, even Giselle!
And she's smiling! For the first time
Since we've arrived! Everyone is
Smiling and laughing except for a few
Who miss their dogs, they can't stand
Not being able to share this moment
With them, and - oh no! Someone has
opened a door, the dogs have come
Streaming in, their eyes are wide, their

Tails are wagging in time to the music,
And they're heading straight for Giselle!

You look over at Cassie but cannot make
Eye contact, it takes all her energy to keep
Squeezing that squeezehox. You try to
Warn Giselle, but she's looking the other
Way, and there are too many dogs and people
In-between for you to reach her. You put
Your hand over your eyes (while still
Dancing), not wanting to see the shock
On Giselle's face when the dogs overtake
Her. And then they do. And she keeps
Dancing! Amazing. But how can that be?

You glance over at the Bride and Groom,
Their bodies are intertwined, there's no
Distance between them, her white gown
And his black suit, they remind you
Of a statue you've seen of Yin and Yang.
You look over at Cassie and smile just as
She looks up and smiles at you. You thank
The universe that you didn't break up with
Her. I mean, what were you even thinking?

COURBET'S BLUE PARROT

I

He perches on the delicately-raised
Left hand of the world's most naked
Woman, gnawing possessively on her
Middle finger, a glint in his left eye, as
She writhes on a rumpled white sheet on
The forest floor in an erotic reverie, her
Long brown hair spread out in tendrils on
The creamy sheet. Her voluptuous body that
Is pleasure itself, pleasure in human form,
Fills the left foreground of Courbet's canvas.

Courbet was 46 when he painted it, already
A rock star of the Parisian art world, the self-
Described "proudest and most arrogant man in
France." He had vowed to get one of his nudes
Into the Academy's Salon who was not a goddess
Or nymph or historical figure. Just a woman. Who
Is doing something extreme enough to outrage
The critics. This was his second try. The first one
Was of two naked women, one going down on the
Other. Exquisitely-painted. But rejected as "trashy."
And then came this woman with the disheveled hair
And the blue parrot on her left hand. Accepted.

II

I saw the painting at the Metropolitan Museum
When I was sixteen, and I didn't like it. Mainly
Because it excited me. Sexually. Oh no. Art wasn't
Supposed to do that, was it? When I stood in front
Of a Titian or a Giorgione, I may be mildly titi-
Lated, but I didn't have to worry about what was
Going on in my nether regions. So I was disturbed.
It was disturbing. And I thought Art was something
Aesthetic, something intellectual, something that

74

Was supposed to make you feel superior to every-
One else, to all the people who didn't spend
Their afternoons in museums, not something that
Seduced you into its fantasy and made you envy
A blue parrot, which this painting definitely did.

III

The right side of Courbet's canvas is dark with a
Rickety twig-thin perch that has a parrot sleeping
On it. Under this darkness (as scholars discovered)
Is a secret: the artist himself, naked. But it was not
The Courbet of that time – full-bearded, bloated by
Booze (which would kill him eleven years later),
The ardent Socialist who would be locked up for
Six months for his anti-Napoleonic beliefs – no,
It was Courbet at 20, as slender and lithe as a Greek
God – Hermes perhaps, or the young Zeus. He is
Standing there, cock out, enraptured by the undulating,
White-skinned young woman with the pear-shaped
Breasts and the blue parrot gnawing on her middle
Finger. Given that the woman writhing in orgasm
Was modeled after the mistress of his middle-age,
What exactly does this reveal? Though maybe the
Question is better-phrased as which came first, the
Male lust or the female seduction? Is the woman's
Erotic bliss a projection of the young painter's libido,
Or was the aging Courbet so stimulated by his own
Creation (as I was when I first saw it!) that he wished
Himself back into his youthful body so he could give
This euphoric woman at her sexual peak a taste of his
Own – transporting them back to the primal situation,
A true Adam and Eve, with full knowledge of
Paradisiacal pleasure (and an infinite capacity to
Achieve it) but without any of the consequent guilt?
Whatever the answer, Courbet painted over this vision
Of his youthful ardor, obscured it with darkness and a
Bird's roosting place. Perhaps he found it too vulgar,

Too obvious, this depiction of erotic attraction? Or
Perhaps he knew that the priggish Academy
Would never go for this idyllic scene of a
Youthful sexual frolic? And that was his
Goal, after all, to beat the Salon at its own
Game by having them display a nude woman
With no mythological or historical ties.
At which the artist succeeded. Though
Four years later he turned down the French
Legion of Honor, just threw it back in their fat
Faces, this proud and arrogant artist who
Followed no other leader than his own muse.

IV

And then there's that blue parrot, with wings
Spread, gnawing so delightedly on his mistress's
Finger. Is he the vanished young Courbet transformed
Into a pet bird by his lover's Circean powers, as some
Art historians have suggested? Perhaps. Of course I
Knew nothing about the image of the youthful artist
Lurking beneath the thick coats of dark paint when I
First saw the painting. Nor did I discover it until many
Years later. Meanwhile I went from being
Disturbed by the canvas to falling in love
With it. Falling deeply deeply in love. It
Exerted a gravitational pull on me, whenever
I stepped into that museum. And of course the
Image of a voluptuous naked woman in ecstasy
Had something to do with that. But more and
More through the years my focus was on that
Blue parrot. He has a male energy, no doubt
About that, with his phallus-shaped head and
That glint in his eye, the way he hovers in mid-
Air and the intensity of his gaze, so laser-focused
On her, his obsession. But for me, he was also my
Way into the painting, into that universe, and how
My imagination could thrive there. Long after I had

Left the gallery and was seated in a crowded train,
Hemmed in on all sides by impatient humanity; or
Else lying in bed that evening, before falling off to
Sleep – I would imagine myself as that blue parrot.
For a time that seems timeless, I would take flight,
Rising in the warm air, as nothing else in my troubled
Life troubled me any longer. I would look down on
That emerald landscape, on those ravishing fields that
Seemed to stretch on forever, as the world
Smelled sweetly around me and my brilliantly-
Colored feathers gleamed in the warm sun.

MORE

EARLY

POEMS

A WILTING ROSE

Our bodies swayed
As a rose full-bloomed —
Sharp brambles blown
Upon night's path;
A trail of thorns
Along black brick
That follows dawn's breeze
To the morning sun.

Shall I remember you then
As an offspring
Of night's breast-white moon?

A swan of sunset burning silver
Upon a still, deserted pond –
Gone with the rise
Of morn's flaming beams?

As dusk's grey bird
Flies into night's blind eye,
Dreams shall flee
Upon seagull's wings
Onto an antique island, We;
There, within a love-red rose
That wilting
To spring's blossom clings –
Shall we
At least in memory be.

1971.

THE IMPORTER OF LOVE

I am the sole inspector
of your ship
and everything you carry
I must see,
from the exotic fashions
of the East
to the Islands' aphrodisiacs.
Your cargo hold
holds wonderful surprises,
tastes that whet
an appetite for passion,
sweet things bound up in sacks.

Your simple things elude me.
I cannot ever count
the ways that you sustain me,
the jasmine rice
you bring in barrels,
or the cinnamon you
send over in sticks.

I cannot ever weigh
your significance,
the book of poems
you found in Mozambique,
the stack of letters
you wrote while you were sick.

Feel free to charge me
Whatever you think is fair.
I charge you only
not to leave me lost and lonely,
not to leave my cupboards bare.

1972.

WOMEN AND WATER

In sleep the other night
I was startled by your breathing,
That swept over my body
And withdrew continually:

I felt the moonlight of your mouth
Upon me, making everything larger,
And I sensed the sympathy of waves
Sweeping me along, an understanding
Of your tides they shared with all
The navigators of your byways.

Then another sound, a different melody
Arose, and I was aware of you and your
Oceanic rhythms as your fingers
Filtered through the ever-shifting sea
And grabbed me by the roots of poetry.

1972.

POEM!

O divine wall-socket!
let me plug
let me plug
let me plug
my restless rocket
into your dark space!
Electrify my face!
My body – shock it!

1975.

BALLOON

My body's a balloon
You blow up big:

Your mouth
Goes to my lips
And puffs one leg
And then another,
Arms, chest, head,
Nose, ears, eyes:

Then your lips go
From my mouth
And up I rise.

1975.

ELEGY FOR A LOST LOVE

So now you are the past
(O wine-dark past!)
And I can be Homeric
In my disregard of you

And all the Illiads and Odysseys
Of our love
That left me lost
(You left me).

You have become
The moments
That I choose
To make of you.

And wasn't it
This definition of Ourselves
We sought
Like scholars?

Though all our deeds
(However epic-making at the time)
Time and Space
Made of no consequence.

1972.

WHAT HAPPENED

You were my life
And that was for the best

Then all that happened
All that happened
Happened all so fast

That I like one
Who on a moving train
Is served a large repast
And mostly ate
What he knew
Would never last
And tried not to think about
What pleased him best,
But just kept eating
More and more
As long as it was there –

Then afterwards recalled us,
You and me,
As two who seemed so close
But were never really more
Than culinary guests.

1973.

THE LOVER

I.

You are the physical world
things I love
their ideal

The space
you fill
is hollowed in my brain

like a sculpture
of pure air
encased in stone.

II

Your skin is
another object, separate:
blue-veined like marble

but as bruised as fruit,
a surface
as impassable as glass.

III

I reach out,
try to touch:
you melt away,

elude me
hiding
like a fever in my blood.

1975.

SCHOOL DANCE

She walks along obedient
Like someone who the teacher sent
To fetch the new boy's medicine.

She doesn't like to walk with men,
But in this case her date's her brother.
Someday she wants to be a mother.
Or so she tells me when we dance.
(Her brother eating, I seize my chance.)

One thing about her I will not miss:
Her punch in my stomach when I sneak a kiss.
But I guess that's just the way it went
As she waltzed away, her message sent.

1975.

BACKGROUND NOISE

While we sipped red wine
and made heartfelt love

five men were murdered
(and all their murders solved)

three couples were divorced
(and two were married)

a Late Night Host gave his monologue
two adults had a talk about STDs

and two people sipped red wine
while making love.

1976.

NIGHT THOUGHTS

baby be my
baby be my
single be my
only be my
go now
if you want it
if you want it
go and
get it
while you want it
you can have it
you can
be there
with my breakfast
with my dinner
with my
ever seen me crying
seen me dying
seen me flying
like a summer
through the shutters
of your camera
when our
lying on the white sand
near the
see,
it's how I told you,
it's quite easy,
it's quite
please don't ever leave me
in the winter
in the summer
in the spring
or in the
fall down
when it hurts you
when the pain begins to numb you

when the time comes
when you have it
when the time comes
then you have it
when the time comes
then the time comes
when the time comes

1977.

THE KISS AT 6 AM

Mouth is a lump of clay
its shape the shapeless
lump your mouth this
morning also is.

("Unfinished sculpture
by Rodin" I think, if
anything unfinished
can still think.)

1977.

REMEMBERING U

Remember:
A seaweed ocean
among foaming breakers
that frothed like dogs.
They nipped at our heels
and licked our feet
for miles and miles
and miles,
panting to keep up with our
panting.

Remember:
babies and old men
were babbling with the wind
like preachers,
wandering the stony
sun-soaked shores
in search of sand-caked sinners.
Their words followed us
into the sheltering dunes,
where we caressed them
and tickled them under their chins.

Remember:
we tamed the ocean's fury
aboard our rolling dinghy
that left creases on the sea,
our lips salty and curled as a pirate's.
Oh yes, we stole that ocean's treasure,
put it in our pleasure chest,
gold doubloons beyond counting
that we could always count again
at our leisure.

Leisure that I never wanted, but am
drowning in now.

1978.

ACKNOWLEDGEMENTS

Special thanks to Howard Kern, ShiftPoetry, Kat Georges and especially Barbara Ligeti for making this book possible. It's hard to be a writer. I treasure my friends and allies.

ABOUT THE AUTHOR

Stephen Fife's two previous poetry collections – *Dreaming in the Maze of Love-Grief-Madness* and *Twisted Hipster* – were published by Cune Press in Seattle. They also published his two memoirs (*Best Revenge: How the Theater Saved My Life and Has Been Killing Me Ever Since* and Amazon bestseller *The 13th Boy: A Memoir of Education and Abuse*), as well as his first novel, *Angel's Glance* – which will be re-issued by Cune Press in August 2022 under the new title *Loving Holly.*

His plays *Savage World, Break of Day* and *This Is Not What I Ordered* – have been published by Samuel French/Concord Theatricals. Other plays include *In The Mood, Sizzle Sizzle, Blue Kiss, The Kitchen Girl, Fun With Freud, Scattered Blossoms, Vincent in the Asylum, Van Gogh's Zombie Movie, New Day, Bring Your Own* and *The Blessing.* His adaptation of Sholem Asch's *God of Vengeance* was produced Off-Broadway and was directed in a revival by Joseph Chaikin. *The American Wife* (co-written with Ralph Pezzullo) had its World Premiere at the Park Theatre in London.

A graduate of Horace Mann H.S., the National Theatre Institute, Sarah Lawrence College and Columbia University's School of the Arts (MFA), Steve has written for The New York Times "Arts and Leisure" section, The Village Voice, American Theatre, Stage Raw (in LA), and The New Republic. He has also edited three volumes of monologues and scenes for Applause Books. He is the recipient of a Federal Poetry grant and has written several screenplays and streaming projects.

Contact Stephen Fife at slfife@aol.com or @twistedhipster8 for further information.